I0825477

BLASTOFF! READERS, AN IMPRINT OF BELLWETHER MEDIA BY FLUTTERBEE

Blastoff! Readers are carefully developed by literacy experts to build reading stamina and move students toward fluency by combining standards-based content with developmentally appropriate text.

LEVELS

Level 1 provides the most support through repetition of high-frequency words, light text, predictable sentence patterns, and strong visual support.

Level 2 offers early readers a bit more challenge through varied sentences, increased text load, and text-supportive special features.

Level 3 advances early-fluent readers toward fluency through increased text load, less reliance on photos, advancing concepts, longer sentences, and more complex special features.

★ **Blastoff! Universe**

Reading Level

Grade K

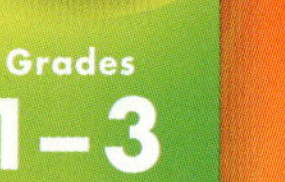

Grades 1–3

Grade 4

This edition first published in 2026 by Bellwether Media, Inc.

For information regarding permission, write to Bellwether Media, Inc., Attention: Permissions Department, 3500 American Blvd W, Suite 150, Bloomington, MN 55431.

Library of Congress Cataloging-in-Publication Data is available at www.loc.gov or upon request from the publisher.

ISBN: 9798893047783 (hardcover)
ISBN: 9798893048780 (ebook)

Editor: Suzane Nguyen Designer: Andrea Schneider

Printed in the United States of America, North Mankato, MN.

Table of Contents

Privyet!

Privyet! My name is Yuri. I speak Russian, or *russkiy yazyk*. Let's learn some words!

Words to Know
•да = yes
da (dah)
•нет = no
net (nyet)
•русский язык = Russian language
russkiy yazyk (ROOS-keey yah-ZEEK)
•меня зовут = my name is
menya zovut (mee-NYAH zah-VOOT)
privyet
(pree-VYEHT)
hello

Russian is spoken in Russia and other countries. The Russian alphabet has 33 letters.

Russian-speaking Countries
Russia

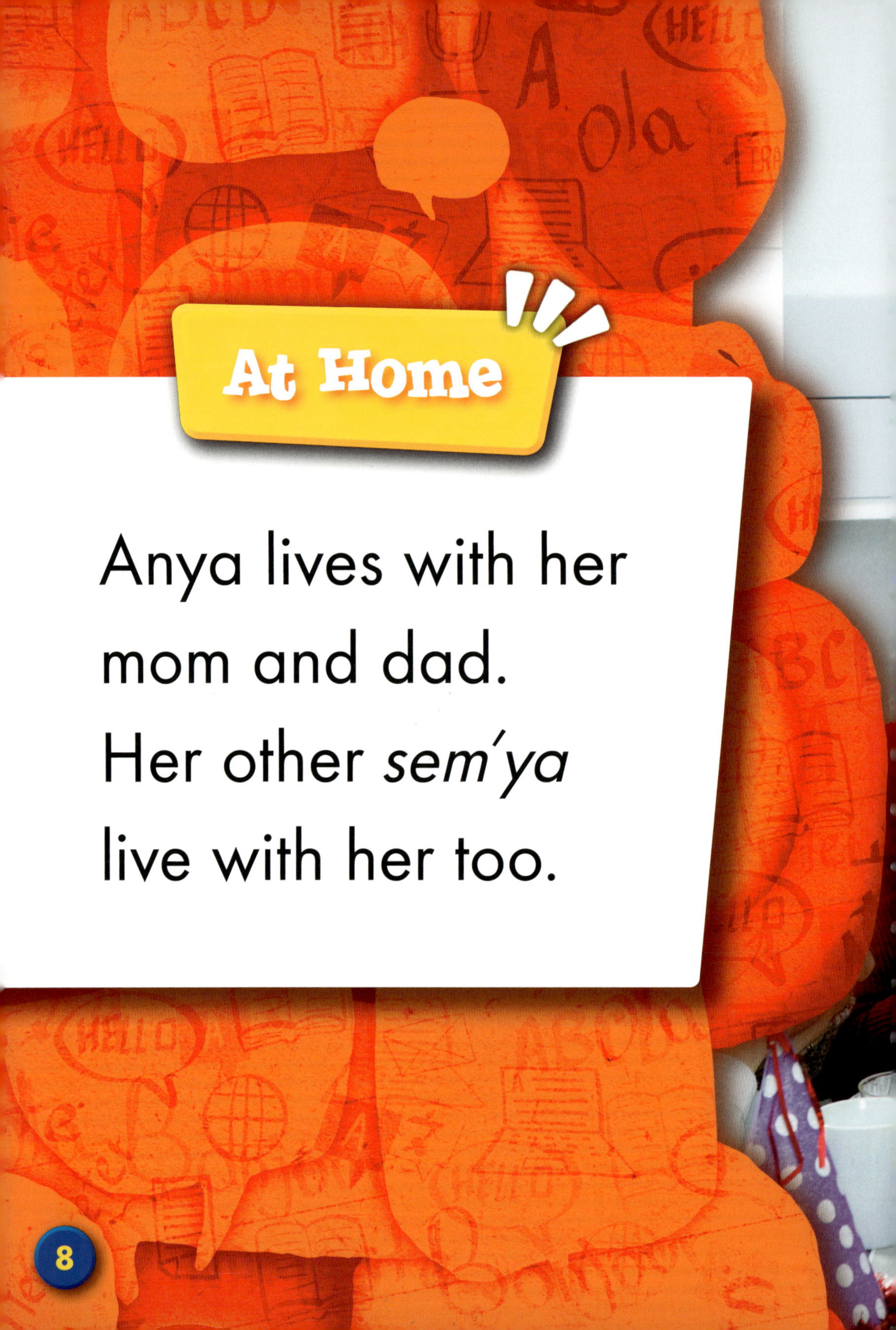

At Home

Anya lives with her mom and dad. Her other *sem'ya* live with her too.

Words to Know
•семья = family
sem'ya (syem'-YAH)
•бабушка = grandma
babushka (BAH-boosh-kah)
•дедушка = grandpa
dedushka (DYEH-doosh-kah)
•сестра = sister
sestra (sees-TRAH)
•брат = brother
brat (braht)
dedushka
babushka

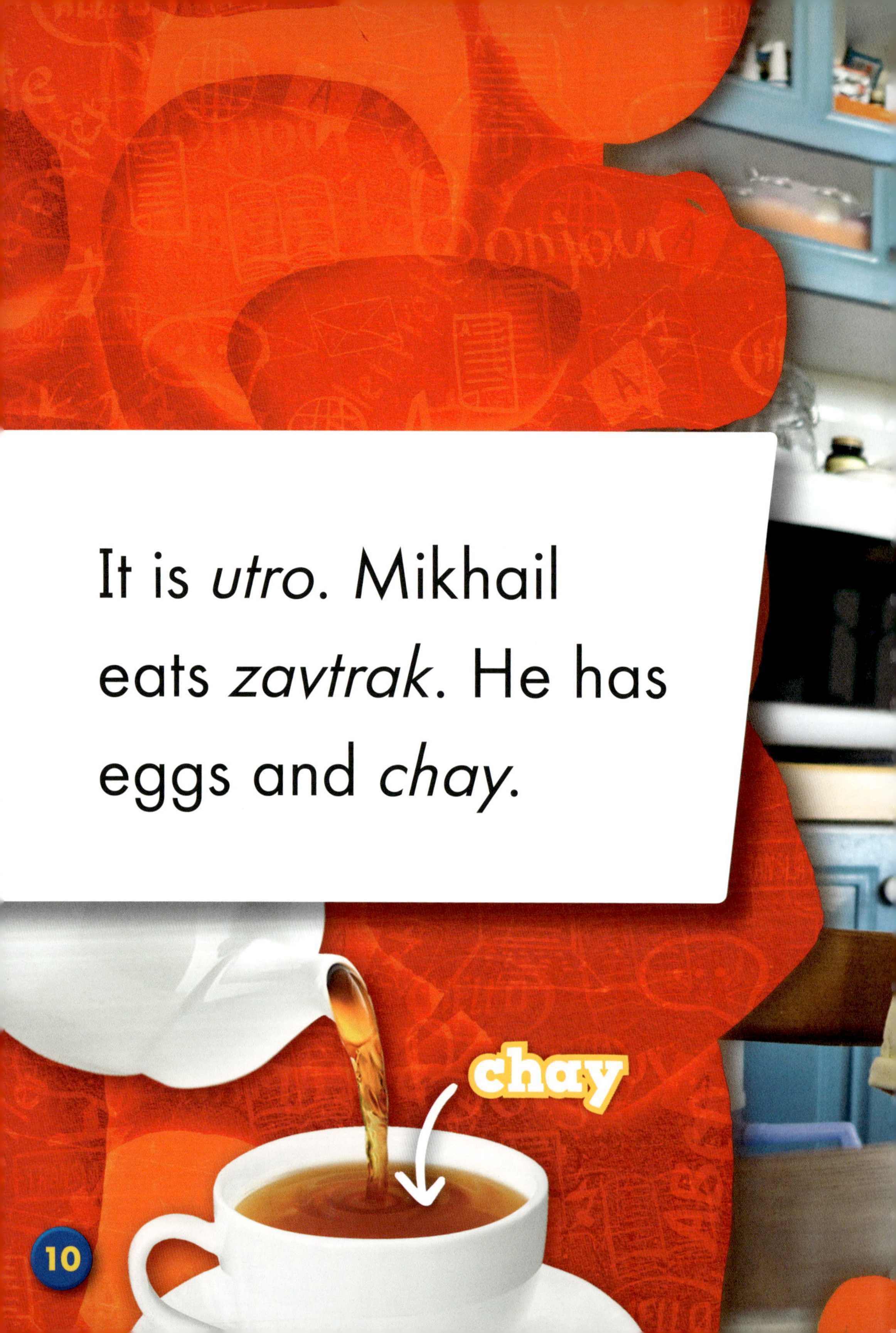

It is *utro*. Mikhail eats *zavtrak*. He has eggs and *chay*.

Words to Know

- утро = **morning**
  utro (OO-trah)
- завтрак = **breakfast**
  zavtrak (ZAHV-trahk)
- чай = **tea**
  chay (chai)
- стол = **table**
  stol (stohl)

At School

Sasha rides her *velosiped* to *shkola*. It is *holodno!*

Words to Know

- велосипед = **bicycle**
  velosiped (veel-eh-see-PYED)
- шлем = **helmet**
  shlem (shlehm)
- школа = **school**
  shkola (SHKOH-lah)
- холодно = **cold**
  holodno (KHOH-lud-nah)
- пальто = **coat**
  pal'to (pahl'-TOH)

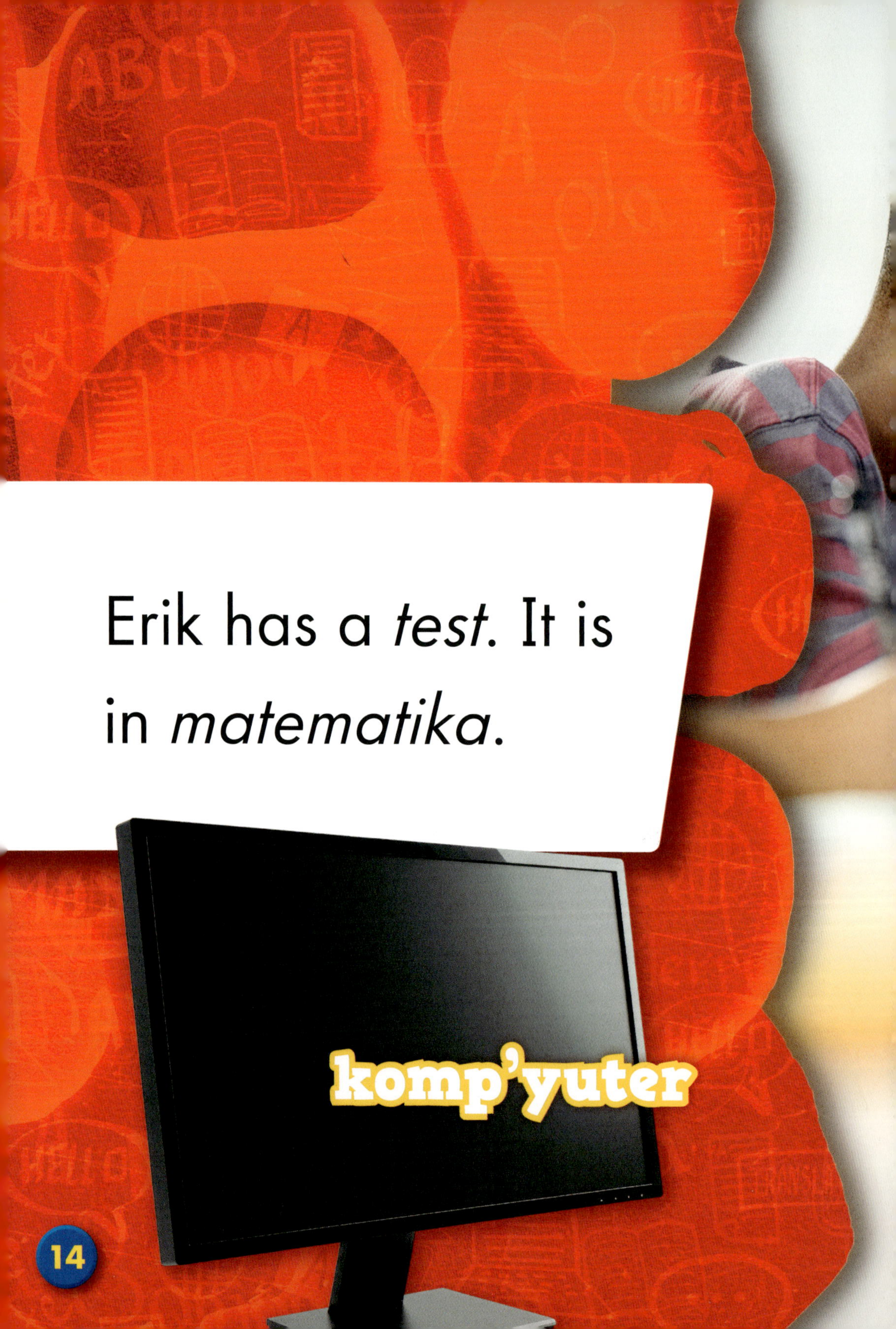

Erik has a *test*. It is in *matematika*.

Count in Russian

один ..... odin (ah-DEEN)... 1

два .... dva (dvah)............ 2

три .... tri (tree).......... 3

четыре...chetyre (cheh-TEE-reh)............... 4

пять ..... pyat' (pyaht')... 5

шесть ... shest' (shest')........ 6

семь ..... sem' (syem')... 7

восемь...vosem' (VOH-syem') 8

девять...devyat' (DYEH-veht')............ 9

десять...desyat' (DYEH-seht')................... 10

karandash

Words to Know

- тест = **test**
  test (tehst)
- математика = **math**
  matematika (mah-tee-MAH-tee-kah)
- карандаш = **pencil**
  karandash (kah-rahn-DAHSH)
- компьютер = **computer**
  komp'yuter (kahm-P'YOO-ter)

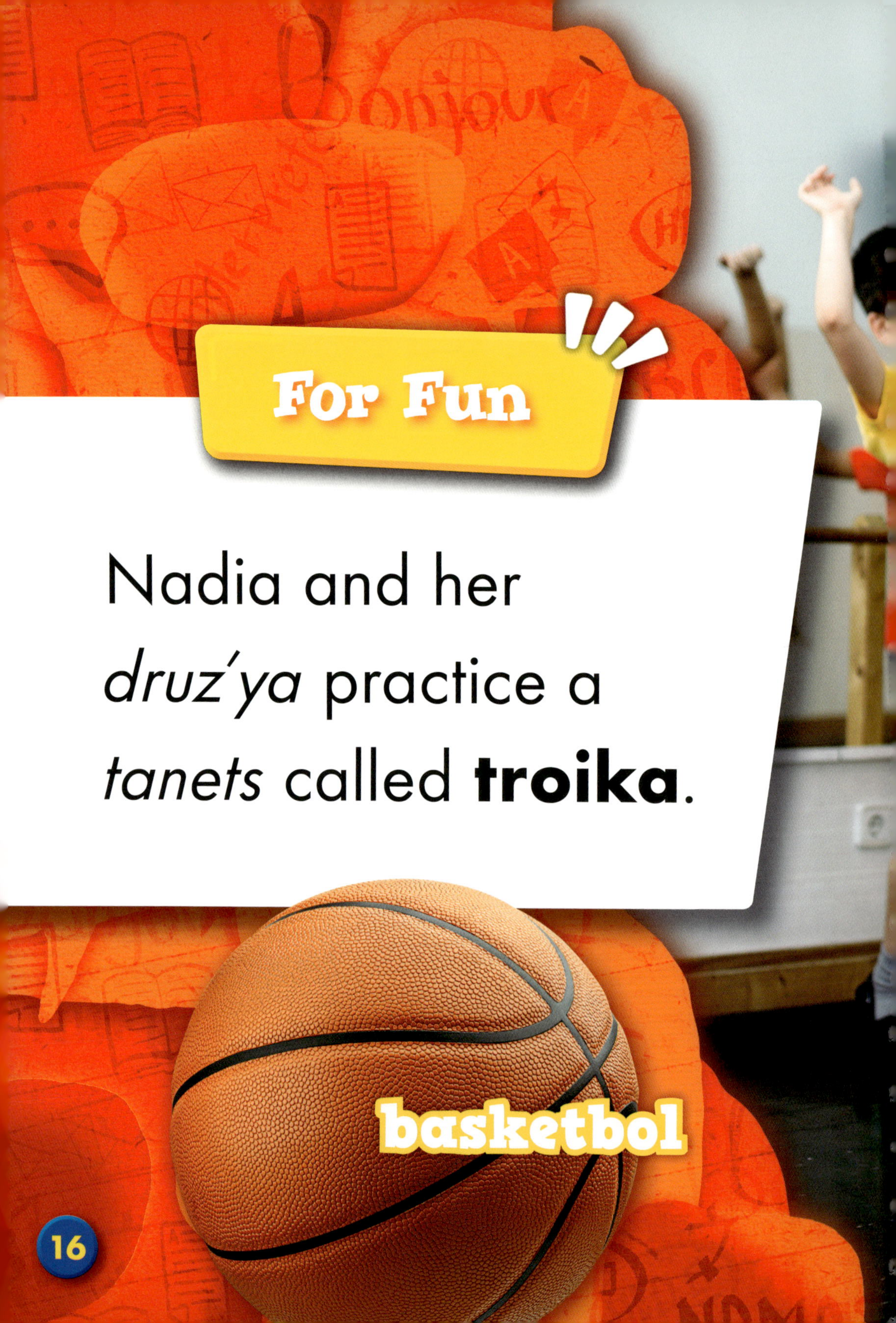

For Fun

Nadia and her *druz'ya* practice a *tanets* called **troika**.

Words to Know

- друзья = **friends**
  druz'ya (droo-Z'YAH)
- танец = **dance**
  tanets (TAH-nyets)
- спорт = **sports**
  sport (sport)
- футбол = **soccer**
  futbol (foot-BOHL)
- баскетбол = **basketball**
  basketbol (bahs-keht-BOHL)

Alina eats *uzhin*.
She likes to eat **blini**.

Words to Know
•ужин = dinner
uzhin (OO-zheen)
•рыба = fish
ryba (REE-bah)
•хлеб = bread
khleb (hlyep)
•тарелка = plate
tarelka (tah-RYEL-kah)
blini

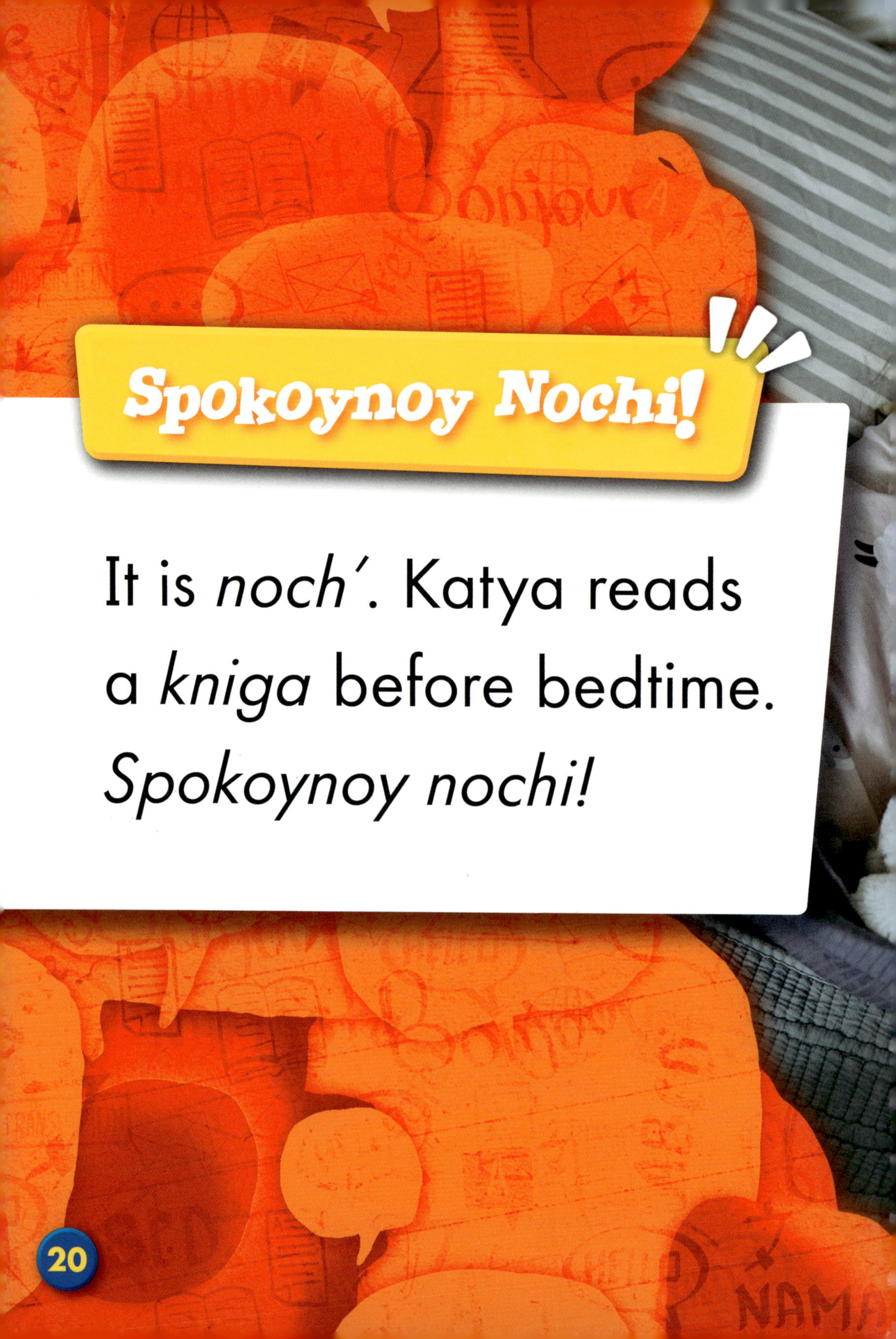

Spokoynoy Nochi!

It is *noch'*. Katya reads a *kniga* before bedtime. *Spokoynoy nochi!*

Words to Know

- ночь = **night**
  noch' (nohch')
- книга = **book**
  kniga (KNEE-gah)
- кровать = **bed**
  krovat' (krah-VAHT')
- подушка = **pillow**
  podushka (pah-DOOSH-kah)

Glossary

blini

thin pancakes eaten with toppings like jam or sour cream

troika

a traditional Russian dance

To Learn More

AT THE LIBRARY

Moening, Kate. *Moscow.* Minneapolis, Minn.: Bellwether Media, 2025.

Sabelko, Rebecca. *Russia.* Minneapolis, Minn.: Bellwether Media, 2023.

Vonder Brink, Tracy. *Russia.* New York, N.Y.: Crabtree Publishing, 2025.

ON THE WEB

FACTSURFER

Factsurfer.com gives you a safe, fun way to find more information.

1. Go to www.factsurfer.com.
2. Enter "Russian" into the search box and click 🔍.
3. Select your book cover to see a list of related content.

Index

The images in this book are reproduced through the courtesy of: famveld/ Alamy Stock Photo, front cover; AlenKadr, p. 3; Tom Wang, pp. 4-5; Mordolff, pp. 6-7; Iakov Filimonov/ Alamy Stock Photo, pp. 8-9; I-MM, p. 10 (chay); JazzIRT/ Getty Images, pp. 10-11; stockphoto-graf, p. 12 (velosiped); pikselstock, pp. 12-13; Paul, p. 14 (komp'yuter); Rido, pp. 14-15; grey, p. 16 (basketbol); JackF, pp. 16-17; Belyaevskiy, p. 18 (khleb); Alex Potemkin, pp. 18-19; Ridofranz, pp. 20-21; lenazap, p. 22 (blini); Fotofabrikanty | Dreamstime.com, p. 22 (troika).